THE BORN LOSER'S GUIDE TO LIFE

ART & CHIP SANSOM

TOPPER BOOKS
AN IMPRINT OF PHAROS BOOKS • A SCRIPPS HOWARD COMPANY
NEW YORK

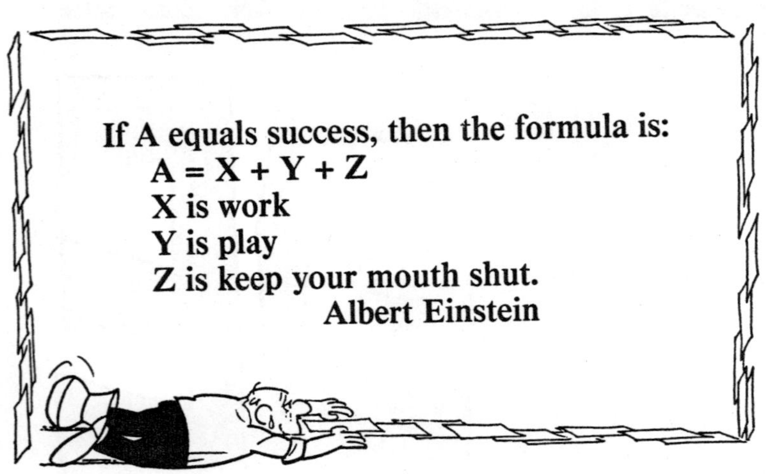
If A equals success, then the formula is:
A = X + Y + Z
X is work
Y is play
Z is keep your mouth shut.
Albert Einstein

Library of Congress Catalog Card Number: 89-043218
Pharos ISBN: 0-88687-597-8

Printed in the United States of America

An Imprint of Pharos Books
A Scripps Howard Company
200 Park Avenue
New York, NY 10166

10 9 8 7 6 5 4 3 2 1

I have been asked to write a few words about Art and Chip Sansom, the creators of THE BORN LOSER comic strip. Frankly, it is impossible for me to be truly objective, because I heartily dislike both of them. After all, they have made me the target of their cheap shots, poked fun at me and hung the horns of the scapegoat on me for 25 years. It *has* been a living, though. Let's face it, without THE BORN LOSER I'd be out of a job and forced to apply for an occasional bit part in a soap opera strip.

So, no hard feelings ... I have a book about *me*, and who ever heard of either Art or Chip Sansom?

—Brutus P. Thornapple

Art Sansom

Chip Sansom

HOME LIFE

SO FAR, SO GOOD.
ART SANSOM 3-29

Life is a joke that's just begun.
W.S. Gilbert

BING
BONG
HE SMIRKED WHEN I SAID I COULD LEARN FRENCH BY CASSETTE.

JE T'ADORE!

YOUR ARM BROKEN? YOU SHUT IT!
9-1

HMM...A FIVE-LETTER WORD STARTING WITH "C," MEANING TO CRAWL STEALTHILY...

THAT'S IT, "CREEP!"
11-1

Woman was God's second blunder.
Nietzche

IT SAYS HERE THAT 75% OF ALL CAR ACCIDENTS OCCUR WITHIN A FIVE-MILE RADIUS OF HOME.

GEE...

MAYBE WE SHOULD MOVE.
© 1984 by NEA Inc

OH, MY, A PIPE!

I LOVE TO SEE A MAN SMOKE A PIPE... IT MAKES HIM LOOK SO DISTINGUISHED AND VIRILE!
© 1980 by NEA, Inc., T.M. Reg. U S Pat Off

IN YOUR CASE, I'LL MAKE AN EXCEPTION.

Fun is fun, but no girl wants to laugh all of the time.

Anita Loos

WHAT'S A MILLENNIUM, BRUTUS?
WELL...

...IT'S SORT OF LIKE A CENTENNIAL... ONLY IT HAS MORE LEGS.
© 1984 by NEA, Inc.

?
DOES THAT SOUND RIGHT TO YOU?
ART SANSOM 7-30

WAIT A MINUTE...

DID YOU EVER HAVE A FEELING OF DÉJÀ VU?

I JUST HAD THE STRONGEST FEELING I'VE BEEN HERE BEFORE!
THIS IS OUR BACK YARD!
ART SANSOM 7-20
© 1984 by NEA, Inc.

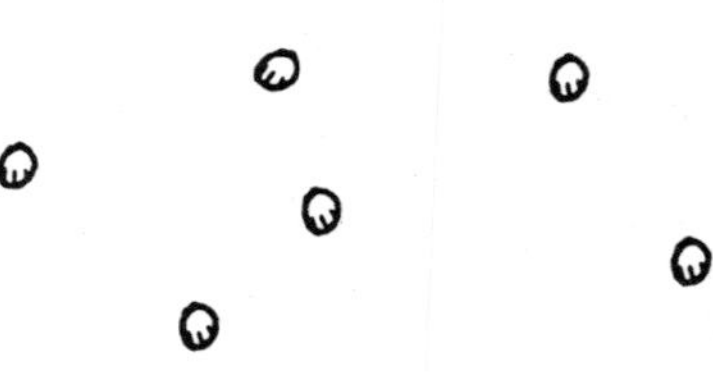

I PLANTED ROSES, BUT EVERYTHING'S COMING UP POTATOES!
ART/chip SANSOM 3-30
© 1987 by NEA, Inc.

GEBBIE PLUMBING.
COME ON IN...
IT'S UPSTAIRS, FIRST DOOR ON THE RIGHT.
GOTCHA!
ART/chip SANSOM
© 1987 by NEA, Inc.
BUBBLE-BUBBLE, TOILET TROUBLE!
I CALL FOR A PLUMBER AND GET THE BARD OF AVON.
9-21

If a thing is worth doing, it's worth doing badly.
Winston Churchill

SIGH...OH, ME...UHHHHHHHHHH
Z
WHAP!
HUH?!
WHAT'S THE MATTER, CAN'T YOU SLEEP EITHER?
YAWN

Never have partners.
Howard Hughes' father

MY WINTER SUIT, GLADYS...THE ONE I SPILLED MAPLE SYRUP ON...YOU FORGOT TO SEND IT TO THE CLEANERS, DIDN'T YOU!

YOU'RE WEIRD, Y'KNOW THAT?
HOW DO YOU FIGURE?
WELL, FOR STARTERS, YOU'VE BEEN SITTING IN FRONT OF THAT TV FOR HOURS!
SO?
TURN IT ON!

The way to be nothing is to do nothing.
Howe

I HATE THESE POWER FAILURES!
YOU CAN SAY THAT AGAIN!
SAY WHAT AGAIN?
I HATE THESE POWER FAILURES.
YOU CAN SAY THAT AGAIN.
© 1987 by NEA, Inc
BOP!
WHAT DID I SAY?

GOOD WORK. I'LL TAKE HIM FROM HERE!

HAS HE GOT A PERMIT FOR THAT THING?

YAWN

DID YOU EVER WAKE UP IN THE MORNING...
© 1988 by NEA, Inc

...AND KNOW IT WAS GOING TO BE A DAY WHEN **NOTHING** COULD GO WRONG?
6-13

WHO'S CRITICIZING YOUR OATMEAL?

I MERELY ASKED FOR A STEAK KNIFE.
2-12

All moanday, tearday, wailsday, thumpsday, frightday, shatterday.

James Joyce

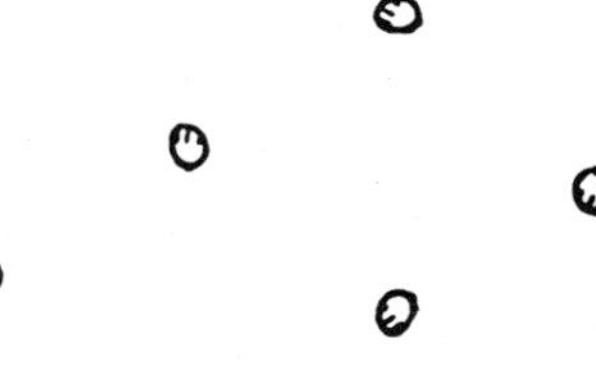

© 1981 by NEA, Inc. TM Reg U.S. Pat. & TM Off
1-1-82
ART SANSOM

IT WON'T BE LONG TILL MIDNIGHT, GLADYS...

YOU'RE RUNNING OUT OF TIME FOR MY SURPRISE BIRTHDAY PARTY!
© 1979 by NEA, Inc. T.M. Reg. U.S. Pat. Off.

YOU WERE EXPECTING ONE?
SURE, YOU DO IT EVERY YEAR!

WELL, THIS YEAR I DECIDED TO SURPRISE YOU. GOOD NIGHT.
ART SANSOM 6-8

Let us respect gray hairs, especially our own.
J.P. Senn

I THINK I'LL START MY VACATION WITH BREAKFAST IN BED, GLADYS! BRING ME TWO THREE-MINUTE EGGS AND RAISIN TOAST!
© 1988 by NEA, Inc.
LET'S MOVE IT, GLADYS, I'M FAMISHED!

KNOW WHY HER PARENTS NAMED HER RAMONA?
© 1988 by NEA, Inc.

BECAUSE THEY COULDN'T SPELL BLEEEEEEECCH!

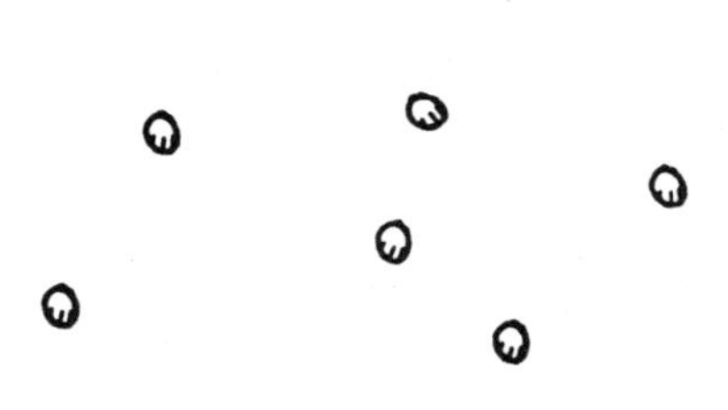

YOU'RE GOING TO LOVE THIS PLACE, FOLKS AND Y'REALLY GOT IT FOR A SONG!

AND THE AIRPORT IS A HANDY THREE BLOCKS AWAY!

5-11

WELL, THAT'S MY SPEECH. THANKS FOR NOT LAUGHING.

10-4

MAYBE EVERYONE'S RIGHT; I DO HAVE TROUBLE EXPRESSING MYSELF.
© 1989 by NEA Inc
8-11

HE SHAVES IN THE SHOWER, EATS INSTANT OATMEAL AND DRINKS INSTANT COFFEE FOR BREAKFAST, SKATEBOARDS TO THE BUS STOP, SPEED-READS THE PAPER ON THE EXPRESS BUS AND STILL CAN'T MAKE IT TO WORK ON TIME!
I'LL SEE YOOOOoooo...
© 1989 by NEA Inc 8-1

THE OFFICE

I love work; it fascinates me. I can sit and look at it for hours.

Jerome K. Jerome

MORNING, ED, T.G.I.F.!

HI, LESTER, T.G.I.F.!

T.G.I.F., MARTHA!
THIS IS THURSDAY.

One of the saddest things is that the thing a man can do for eight hours a day, day after day, is work. You can't eat for eight hours a day nor drink for eight hours a day nor make love eight hours a day —all you can do for eight hours is work.

William Faulkner

HOWDY, CHIEF!
R.W. VEEBLEFESTER
NOW HEAR THIS!
PRE$IDENT

HERE I AM, BACK FROM MY GLORIOUS TWO-WEEK TROPICAL VACATION!
R.W. VEEBLEFESTER
NOW HEAR THIS!
PRE$IDENT
© 1989 by NEA, Inc

YOU'VE BEEN AWAY?
R.W. VEEBLEFESTER
NOW HEAR THIS!
PRE$IDENT
1-30

I'LL WANT YOUR INPUT REGARDING THE NEW AD CAMPAIGN...

I'M CALLING A MEETING FOR TEN TOMORROW TO DISCUSS IT...MEANWHILE, SLEEP ON IT!
© 1989 by NEA, Inc

Z Z
NOT NOW!
4-15

Diplomacy is to do and say
The nastiest thing in the nicest way.
Isaac Goldberg

IT'S WHACKER, SIR, HE'S THREATENING TO JUMP!

TRY NOT TO LAND ON THE SILVER MERCEDES...
©1982 by NEA, Inc. TM Reg U.S. Pat. & TM Off.
10-5

I'M OVERDUE FOR A RAISE, AND I DEMAND CONSIDERATION NOW! THIS IS IT! I'M GOING TO COUNT TO TEN--
1983 by NEA, Inc. TM Reg U.S. Pat. & TM Off.
NO SENSE IN TRYING TO SHOW OFF NOW...I'M WELL AWARE OF YOUR LIMITATIONS.
6-24

The only way to succeed is to make people hate you. That way, they remember you.
Joseph von Sternberg

NAME?
FRANK LLOYD.

FRANK... LLOYD...
RIGHT!

© 1987 by NEA, Inc.

THOSE IN FAVOR SAY "AYE."
"AYE."

"NAY."
THE "NAY'S" HAVE IT.
© 1980 by NEA, Inc. T.M. Reg U.S. Pat Off

It's always been and will always be in the world: the horse does the work, and the coachman gets tipped.

Anonymous

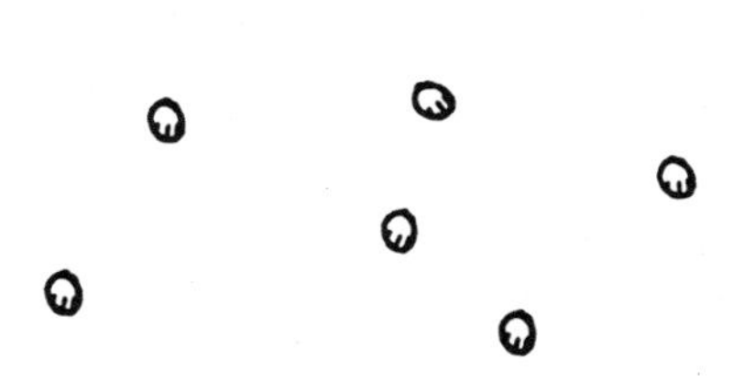

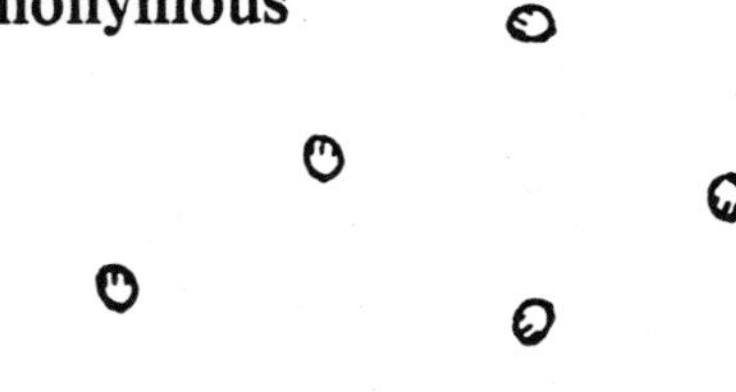

WOW, YOU LOOK LIKE YOU MUST HAVE JUST CLOSED A BIG DEAL!

I HAVE INDEED! JUST PURCHASED A RENOIR FOR MY WIFE'S BIRTHDAY!

HOW ABOUT THAT HYPOCRITE! HE PREACHES "BUY AMERICAN," THEN GOES OUT AND GETS A FOREIGN CAR!
1-30

1983 by NEA Inc TM Reg U S Pat & TM Off

MEN CAN FIND THEIR WAY TO THE MOON...... HE GETS LOST ON HIS WAY TO THE WASHROOM.
2-17

Nice guys finish last.
Leo Durocher

YOU NEVER CALL UPON MY EXPERTISE WHEN DECISIONS ARE MADE!

NEXT IDEA YOU HAVE, TRY BOUNCING IT OFF ME!

SQUEAKY WHEEL GETS THE GREASE!
©1986 by NEA, Inc.

EVERYONE SAYS HOW GREAT JANE FONDA VIDEOS ARE TO WORKOUT TO...

BUT I COULDN'T SEEM TO GET THE HANG OF IT.
YEAH? WHICH ONE DID YOU RENT?
"KLUTE"
© 1985 by NEA, Inc.

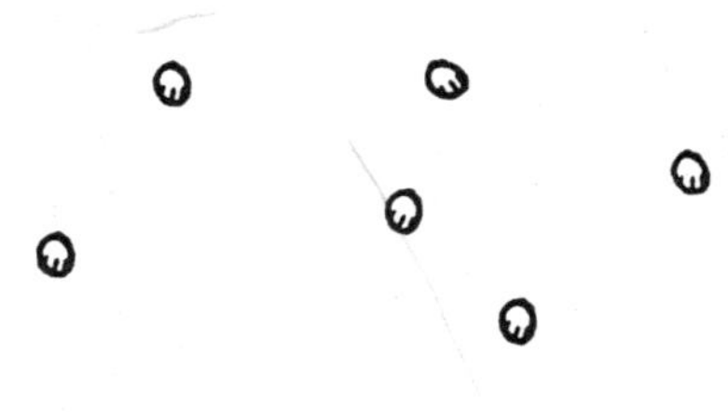

CLOSE THAT WINDOW, SOMEBODY! D'YA HEAR ME!

WHAT ARE YOU DOING?

SITTING ON THESE PAPERS SO THEY WON'T BLOW AWAY.

I THINK I'VE FOUND HIS NICHE... HE'S A PAPERWEIGHT.

CONFOUND IT, WHY DO YOU ALWAYS CRITICIZE MY WORTH AROUND HERE?

AFTER ALL, YOU SAID YOU TAUGHT ME EVERYTHING YOU KNOW!

CORRECTION... I SAID, I TAUGHT YOU EVERYTHING **YOU** KNOW.

Truth is the safest lie.
Yiddish proverb

I'M APPLYING FOR YOUR JOB OPENING.
I SEE... SPELL YOUR NAME...
P-E-T-E-R P-F-E-I-F-F-E-R, THE "P" IS SILENT.
NICE TO MEET YOU, ETER.
© 1985 by NEA, Inc
REMEMBER, I AM THE BOSS BECAUSE I AM SMARTER THAN ANY OF YOU!
I AM A PHI BETA KAPPA, SIR.
YOU'RE FIRED!

Never drink beer at your desk. Supervisors don't like it.

Ian Shoales

EX
IT

FINISHED ALREADY? GOOD WORK!
EX
IT

I FEARED YOU MIGHT BOTCH IT.
ENTR
IT
Art Sansom
© 1985 by NEA Inc 6-7

NO! NONONONONONONO! ONE MORE WHIMPERING SQUEAL OUT OF YOU ABOUT A RAISE AND YOU'RE DEAD IN THE WATER! NOW GET OUT!

YOU KNOW, THERE ARE TIMES WHEN I DON'T LIKE MYSELF VERY MUCH...

...BUT THEN, THERE ARE TIMES LIKE THIS THAT MAKE IT ALL WORTHWHILE!
Art/Chip Sansom 6-20
© 1987 by NEA, Inc.

The only place success comes before work is in the dictionary.

Vidal Sassoon

NO "BUTS," SISTER, I'M WAITING HERE TILL HE RETURNS!
IT'S BEEN TWO HOURS! WHERE IS HE?!
ON VACATION.

HA-HA, I HEARD A REAL GASSER TODAY! SAY KNOCK-KNOCK...
KNOCK-KNOCK.
WHO'S THERE?
!
©1986 by NEA, Inc.

Clever liars give details, but the cleverest don't.
Anonymous

I DON'T BELIEVE IT! CAN IT BE THAT HE'S DEEP IN THOUGHT...

...BRAINSTORMING SOME BRILLIANT NEW MARKETING STRATEGY...

...OR JUST CATCHING UP ON HIS SLEEP?

MY BOY, I'VE DECIDED TO MAKE YOU A FULL PARTNER AT A HUGE SALARY INCREASE!
SEE YOU AROUND.

WHERE ARE YOU GOING?

I'M IN THE WRONG GAG.
©1986 by NEA, Inc.

I always go where the dough is.
Gypsy Rose Lee

Doing nothing—that's hard work.
John Fowles

I AM PRESENTING YOU THIS WATCH COMMEMORATING YOUR SERVICE TO THE COMPANY!

BUT IT'S NOT WORKING...
© 1987 by NEA, Inc.

LIKE I SAID...
ART/chip SANSOM 1-9-88

FIVE O'CLOCK ALREADY! WHERE HAS THE DAY GONE?

FIVE O'CLOCK ?!

MENTION QUITTING TIME AND HE CAN MOVE FASTER THAN ANY FAT MAN ON EARTH!
© 1985 by NEA, Inc
4-15

He who can lick can bite.
French proverb

KIDS

HURRICANE HATTIE O'HARA? WHY, YES, A DELIGHTFUL YOUNGSTER...
LIVES RIGHT HERE IN THE NEIGHBORHOOD... MATTER OF FACT, JUST A STONE'S TH—
© 1988 by NEA, Inc

Raising kids is part joy and part guerilla warfare.

Ed Asner

HEY, POP, Y'WANTA ARM RASSLE?
SURE...

WOULDN'T YOU RATHER DO THIS WITH ONE OF YOUR LITTLE FRIENDS?

THEY CAN ALL TAKE ME.
© 1988 by NEA, Inc.

KNOW WHAT WOULD BE NICE...
...IF YOU RAN NEXT DOOR TO SEE HOW OLD MRS. VELVICK IS.

WELL?
SHE SAYS HOW OLD SHE IS IS NONE OF YOUR BEESWAX.

Children are natural mimics—they act like their parents in spite of every attempt to teach them good manners.

Anonymous

YOUR SHOE'S UNTIED, BRUTUS!

?
© 1978 by NEA, Inc., T.M. Reg. U.S. Pat. Off.

GOT'CHA!
5-8

HAVE A GOOD TIME AT FUNLAND?
A GOOD TIME? I GOT SOAKIN' WET IN THE CRUMMY TUNNEL OF LOVE!

HEH-HEH, THE BOAT SINK?

THERE'S A BOAT?
© 1988 by NEA, Inc
3-14

There is always a moment in childhood when the door opens and lets the future in.
Graham Greene

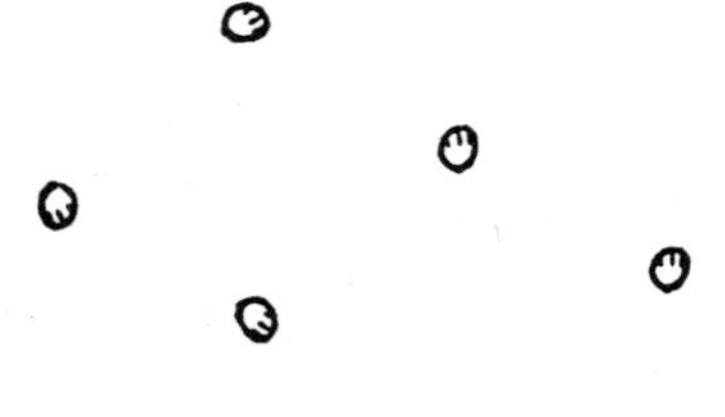

I'LL TELL YOU WHY I'M SITTING DOWN! I'M SITTING DOWN BE-CAUSE IT'S MORE CONVENIENT!
IT SO HAPPENS THAT MICHELANGELO PAINTED THE SISTINE CHAPEL ON HIS BACK!
?
DIDN'T IT WASH OFF WHEN HE WENT SWIMMING?
ART SANSOM 9-20

WHAT'S THE NAME OF THE KID WHO BEAT YOU UP?
I DON'T KNOW.
CAN YOU DESCRIBE HIM?
HECK, YES...
IN FACT, THAT'S WHY HE BEAT ME UP.
ART SANSOM 1-19

A little rebellion now and then is a good thing.
Thomas Jefferson

YOU KIDS SPEND SO MUCH TIME GLUED TO TV SETS...
© 1989 by NEA, Inc.

...DO YOU HAVE THE FOGGIEST NOTION OF WHAT MAKES THEM WORK?
Y'MEAN YOU DON'T?
WELL, UH, I HAVE TO ADMIT I DON'T...
THAT LITTLE KNOB ON TH' LEFT... Y'JUST PUSH IT.

CHIN UP, KIDS!
WE'RE ONLY DOWN BY 15 RUNS.
COACH
BUGS

YOGI BERRA SAID, "IT'S NOT OVER TILL IT'S OVER."
COACH
BUGS
© 1989 by NEA, Inc.

GREAT, WE'RE GETTIN' SKUNKED AND OUR COACH STARTS QUOTIN' CARTOON CHARACTERS!
BUGS

Having a family is like having a bowling alley installed in your brain.

Martin Mull

I DON'T THINK OUR TURN INDICATOR IS WORKING... HOP OUT AND CHECK IT...

WELL...? IS IT ON?

NO
YES
NO
YES
NO
8-26 © 1985 by NEA Inc

WE'RE GOING TO HAVE TO GET THE GLOVES OUT AND TEACH YOU THE MANLY ART.

WHEN I WAS IN THE SECOND GRADE, I COULD WHIP EVERY KID IN THE CLASS!
© 1983 by NEA, Inc. TM Reg U.S. Pat & TM Off

THAT'S BECAUSE DADDY WAS 14 YEARS OLD.

Parents are the bones on which children cut their teeth.

Peter Ustinov

HAH, THIS IS NOTHING, MY BOY. WHEN I WAS YOUR AGE, IT SNOWED TO THE TOP OF MY HEAD!
ART SANSOM
2-7
© 1980 by NEA, Inc., T.M. Reg. U. S. Pat. Off.

IT'S ALL RIGHT, DEAR, JUST STEP ON AND IT WILL CARRY YOU UP TO THE NEXT FLOOR.
I'M NOT GOIN' UP.
I'M WAITIN' FOR MY CHEWIN' GUM T'COME BACK.
© 1982 by NEA, Inc., TM Reg. U.S. Pat. & TM Off.
ART SANSOM
11-22

Familiarity breeds contempt—and children.
Mark Twain

HEY, THAT'S PRETTY GOOD...
PACHYDƎRM
...BUT YOU MISSPELLED ELEPHANT, MY BOY!
!
© 1985 by NEA, Inc.
4-22
SANSOM

THAT'S FUNNY, I DON'T HEAR ANYTHING...
WHY DON'T'CHA TRY TAKIN' THAT STUPID SHELL OUTA YOUR EAR?
© 1981 by NEA, Inc. TM Reg U S Pat & TM Off
SANSOM
9-11

First you have to teach a child to talk, then you have to teach it to be quiet.

Herbert V. Prochnow

DID YOU KNOW THAT "SUGAR" IS THE ONLY WORD IN THE ENGLISH LANGUAGE THAT BEGINS WITH "SU" AND IS PRONOUNCED "SHU"?
SURE.

© 1982 by NEA, Inc. TM Reg U.S. Pat. & TM Off

IT'S TIME YOU LEARNED TO DEFEND YOURSELF LIKE A MAN!

NOW WHAT'S THE FIRST THING YOU'D DO IF A BULLY PICKED ON YOU?

Many a family tree needs trimming.
Frank McKinney Hubbard

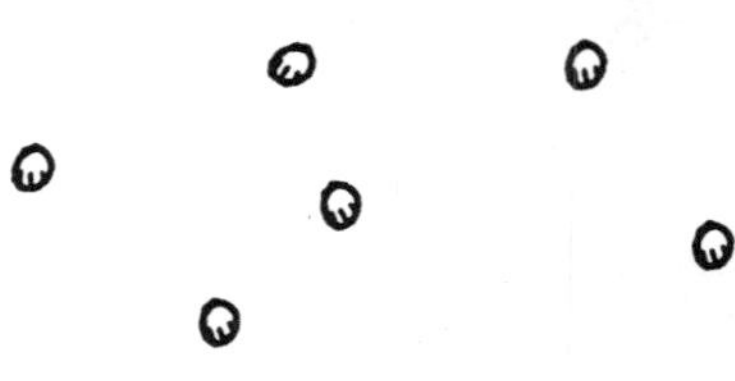

I'M DIRTIER THAN YOU ARE, BOY!

WELL, SURE...
© 1983 by NEA, Inc., TM Reg U S Pat & TM Off
PAT SANSOM

...YOU'RE SIX MONTHS OLDER THAN ME.
3-10

I DON'T GET IT...

...THEY PUT'CHA TO BED WHEN YOU'RE NOT TIRED...
© 1988 by NEA, Inc

...AND WAKE YOU UP WHEN YOU'RE SLEEPY.
10-6

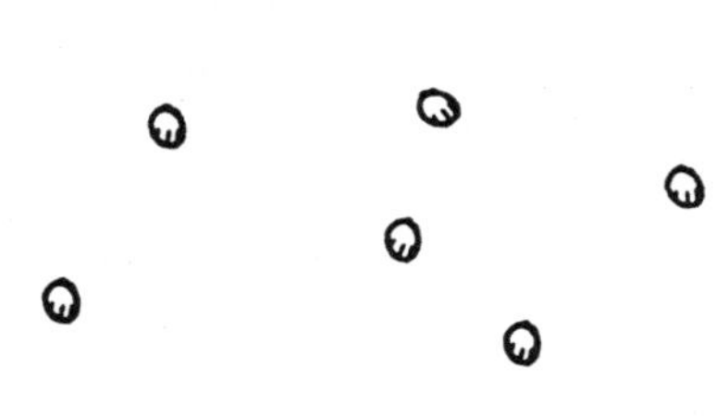

SPORTS

NOW I'M GOING TO TEACH YOU THE SERVE...
OKEYDOKE!
TAKE YOUR RACKET IN ONE HAND AND THE BALL IN THE OTHER...
NOW TOSS IT IN THE AIR...
THE BALL, GLADYS!
© 1989 by NEA Inc
10-6

Show me a good loser, and I'll show you a loser.
Jimmy Carter

WOW! MY FIRST GOOD DRIVE OF THE YEAR!
②PAR 4 395
© 1980 by NEA, Inc., T.M. Reg. U.S. Pat. Off

I CAN'T HIT, I CAN'T THROW, AND I CAN'T FIELD!
YEAH?
WELL Y'BETTER PRACTICE, OR THEY'LL BOOT YA OFF THE TEAM!
THEY CAN'T...
...I'M THE STAR.
© 1989 by NEA, Inc

Experience is the name everyone gives to his mistakes.

Oscar Wilde

GOLF IS 80% HUMOR, TRAGEDY, MELODRAMA, CUSSEDNESS AND CONVER-SATION...
© 1981 by NEA, Inc. TM Reg U.S. Pat & TM Off

...AND ONLY 20% MECHANICS AND TECHNIQUE. GRANTLAND RICE SAID THAT.

HE MUST HAVE PLAYED WITH YOU.
7-10

THESE LESSONS ARE GOING TO GET ME OFF ON THE RIGHT FOOT THIS YEAR.
PRO
PRACTICE TEE

WHAT TIP CAN YOU GIVE ME TO CHOP A FEW STROKES OFF MY SCORE CARD?
5/14
© 1982 by NEA, Inc. TM Reg U.S. Pat & TM Off

ERASER.
PRO

If there is any larceny in a man, golf will bring it out.

Paul Gallico

ALL RIGHT, MEN, NOW COME OUT FIGHTING AND SHAKE HANDS!
© 1985 by NEA, Inc

ZONK

...OR IS THAT, "SHAKE HANDS AND COME OUT FIGHTING"?

GOT PLANS FOR THE WEEKEND?
GOING SKEET-SHOOTING.

DID'JA EVER HIT ANY?
OF COURSE...
© 1987 by NEA, Inc

THEY GOOD EATING?

A man who has no imagination has no wings.
Muhammed Ali

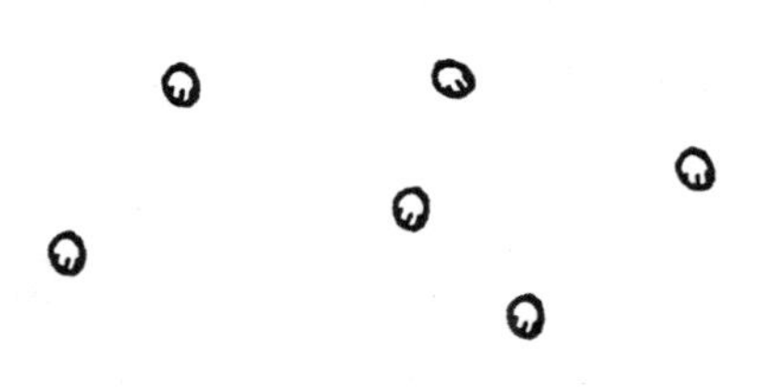

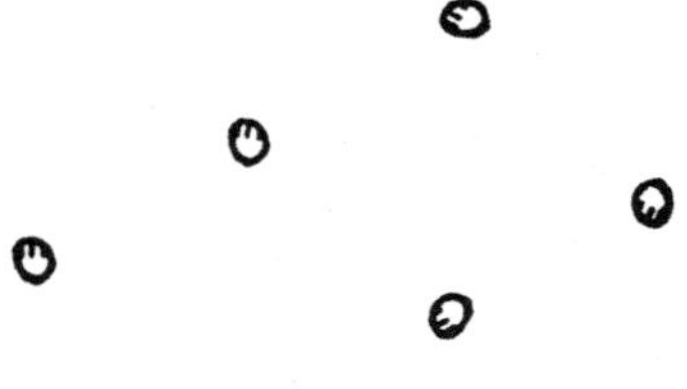

FOR STARTERS, LET ME SEE YOU ADDRESS THE BALL...
?
ALL RIGHT.
PRO
PRACTICE RANGE

LET'S SEE IF I HAVE A PEN...
PRO
PRACTICE RANGE
© 1986 by NEA, Inc.
7-18

DID THE PRO STRAIGHTEN OUT YOUR PROBLEMS?
HE SAID TO PRACTICE MY SWING AT HOME IN FRONT OF THE MIRROR.

CRASH!

NOT WITH A BALL!
© 1987 by NEA, Inc
9-11

The worst men often give the best advice.
P.J. Bailey

GOTTA START PUTTING MORE MUSTARD ON IT.
© 1986 by NEA, Inc

HERE'S THE $5 I OWE YOU FROM OUR ROUND OF GOLF.

YOU WON FIVE BUCKS FROM THE OLD MAN PLAYING GOLF?!

I CADDIED FOR HIM.

The bowling alley is the poor man's country club.

Sanford Hansell

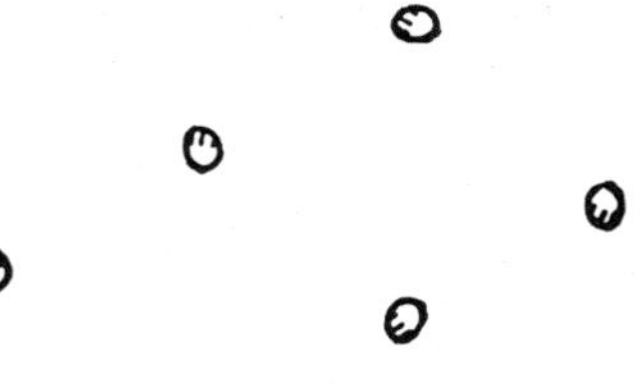

I'D SUGGEST A SADDLE WITH A HORN, MA'AM.

CAN'T I JUST GO "BEEP-BEEP?"

I SHOULD HAVE STAYED BACK HOME ON THE RANGE.
© 1978 by NEA, Inc., T.M. Reg. U.S. Pat. Off.
1-16

YO, BRUTUS! WHERE YA GOIN'?

FLY FISHING!
© 1989 by NEA, Inc.
6-30

I THINK HE'S FINALLY CRACKED.

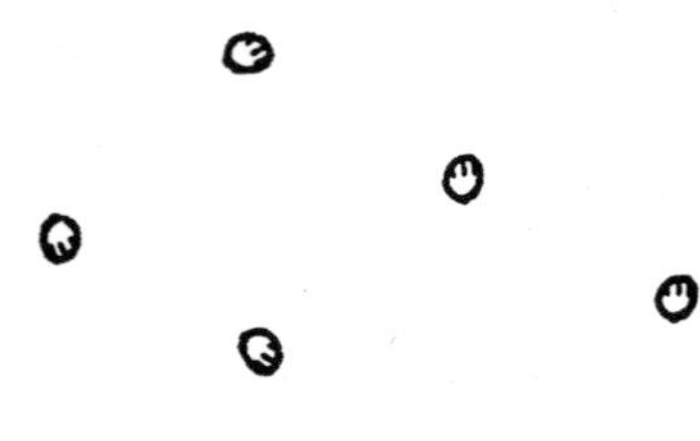

PLAY GOLF OVER THE WEEKEND?
YEAH.

I ALMOST MADE A HOLE IN ONE ON THE THIRD HOLE!
REALLY? WHICH ONE IS THAT?
© 1983 by NEA, Inc. TM Reg U.S. Pat & TM Off

THE ONE WHERE YOU PUTT UP THE DRAWBRIDGE AND THROUGH THE LITTLE CASTLE!
8/8

OH, MY, YES, I WAS PRACTICALLY RAISED ON A BOAT, BUT NOT MY WIFE, GLADYS... I SWEAR SHE DOESN'T EVEN KNOW WHICH SIDE IS PORT AND WHICH SIDE IS SHERRY!
© 1983 by NEA, Inc. TM Reg U.S. Pat & TM Off
4-18

THE OBJECT IS TO HIT THE BALL INTO THAT HOLE WITH THE FLAG.
① PAR 4 395
I GET IT...
...AND YOU'RE SUPPOSED T'TRY TO STOP ME, RIGHT?
© 1984 by NEA, Inc.

DON'T WORRY ABOUT ME CATCHING THE BALL, GLADYS, I CAN CATCH ANYTHING YOU CAN THROW!
© 1988 by NEA, Inc.
LET'S SEE WHAT KIND OF AN ARM YOU'VE GOT, HA-HA!

Winning isn't everything, but wanting to win is.
Vince Lombardi

CRUMMY, MISERABLE, FRUSTRATING GAME ...BEEN PLAYING FOR 20 YEARS AND STILL CAN'T BREAK 100!

I HATE THE TEES, I HATE THE ROUGHS, I HATE THE FAIRWAYS, I HATE THE GREENS...
PRO SHOP
I NEED A STARTING TIME FOR TOMORROW, HARRY.
© 1982 by NEA, Inc. TM Reg U S Pat & TM Off
9-1

AND THEY CALL ME THE "BORN LOSER"!
© 1983 by NEA, Inc. TM Reg U S Pat & TM Off

6-1

Sports is like a war without the killing.
Ted Turner

Man errs as long as he strives.
Goethe

CHANCE ENCOUNTERS

OH, WHAT A BEAUTIFUL MORNING...

OH, WHAT A BEAUTIFUL DAY...

THIS ONE'S MINE, LEONARD...

now and then
there is a person born
who is so unlucky
that he runs into accidents
which started out to happen
to somebody else.
Don Marquis

OOPS! SORRY!

SONOFAGUN! THAT JOKER LIFTED MY WALLET!

WELL, THE JOKE'S ON HIM...

I HIDE MY MONEY IN MY HATBAND!

CARE TO CONTRIBUTE TO THE GEORGE A. GLOCK HOME FOR THE FEEBLE-MINDED?
WHY NOT?

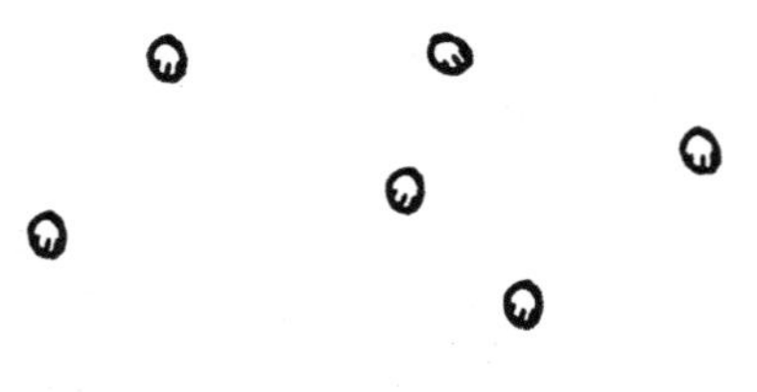

ASK ME IF I'M A GRAPE! GO AHEAD, ASK ME!
?
ARE YOU A GRAPE ?
BUS

YES...NOW ASK ME IF I'M A CUMQUAT.
ARE YOU A CUMQUAT?
BUS
© 1979 by NEA, Inc. T.M. Reg U.S. Pat Off

NO, I ALREADY SAID I'M A GRAPE!
IN A PIG'S EYE YOU ARE!
BUS
9-27

?

"KEEP OUR CITY CLEAN!"
© 1984 by NEA, Inc

IT'S ABOUT TIME THEY DID SOMETHING ABOUT LITTERING!
CHIP + BROOKE
RAVERS RULE!
10-27

PSST...HERE'S MY PHONE NUMBER...
BUS
© 1986 by NEA, Inc.

DON'T LOSE IT, IT'S UNLISTED...
BUS

I DON'T WANT ANY WEIRDOS BOTHERIN' ME!
BUS

BRING ME A BANANA DAIQUIRI...

NOT TILL YOU REMOVE THE SKIS!
© 1989 by NEA, Inc
8-29

BEG PARDON...MIGHT I GO AHEAD OF YOU?
NO!
OH, DEAR, NOW I SHALL BE LATE FOR MY ADVANCED "KUNG FU" CLASS!

1-9-86

I'LL HAVE A HALF POUND OF SALAMI.
WE DON'T CARRY IT.
THEN GIVE ME A HALF POUND OF PASTRAMI.
WE DON'T CARRY IT.
HOW ABOUT CORNED BEEF?
DON'T CARRY IT.
THIS IS **SOME DELI!**
THIS IS A HARDWARE STORE.

We love a joke that hands us a pat on the back while it kicks the other fellow downstairs.
C.L.Edson

WHY DON'T WE JUST STOP AND GIVE THE MUGGER OUR MONEY?
NO!

BUT YOU CAN'T POSSIBLY OUTRUN HIM!
I DON'T HAVE TO...

I ONLY HAVE TO OUTRUN YOU.
© 1984 by NEA Inc

HOLD IT, SAM, I'M OUT OF GAS!

GOOD THING I HAPPENED ALONG WITH MY SIPHON...
!
GAS

MAN, I HOPE I NEVER GET THAT THIRSTY!
© 1984 by NEA, Inc.

Of the thirty-six ways of avoiding disaster, running away is best.

Chinese proverb

Men willingly believe what they will.

Julius Caesar

I WANT TO RETURN THIS "DO-IT-YOURSELF" BOOK!

LOOK, ALL THE PAGES ARE BLANK!
SO?

THINK ABOUT IT.

I CAN SEE INTO THE FUTURE!
YEAH, SURE...
BUS STOP

WHAT TIME IS IT?
5:30
BUS STOP

IN A HALF HOUR IT WILL BE SIX O'CLOCK!
BUS STOP

If you don't know what it is, don't mess with it.
Fats Waller

MY CAR HAS BEEN STOLEN! IT WAS PARKED RIGHT DOWN THE STREET!

WHAT KIND IS IT?

A COMPACT... WINE COLORED...
© 1987 by NEA, Inc.

RED OR WHITE?

AT LEAST I DID BETTER THAN YOU DID ON THE TEST.

WHADAYA MEAN? YOU MISSED ALL THE QUESTIONS, TOO!

I DIDN'T MISSPELL MY NAME.

MAY I HAVE YOUR AUTOGRAPH?... OH, I'M SORRY, I THOUGHT YOU WERE PAUL NEWMAN.
BUS

BUS

MAY I HAVE YOUR AUTOGRAPH?... OH, I'M SORRY, I THOUGHT YOU WERE PAUL NEWMAN.
BUS

"IDLENESS IS EMPTINESS. THE TREE IN WHICH SAP IS STAGNANT REMAINS FRUITLESS." —HOSEA BALLOU
!

"STICKS AND STONES MAY BREAK MY BONES, BUT NAMES CAN NEVER HURT ME." —MOTHER GOOSE

OCCASION-
ALLY I
WIN ONE.
1-6-82

© 1989 by NEA, Inc
10-9
EXPRESS LANE
12 ITEMS OR LESS

A laugh is worth a hundred groans in any market.

Lamb

WINDY T'DAY, AIN'T IT, HIRAM?
HOWZAT?
WINDY! WINDY!
NOPE, IT'S THURSDAY.
ME, TOO, LET'S GO GET A BANANA DAIQUIRI.
BUS
BUS
BUS

HEY, AREN'T YOU THE ONE THEY CALL "THE BORN LOSER"?
BUS
CERTAINLY NOT!
BUS
I COULD HAVE SWORN YOU WERE.
BUS

Forgive, O Lord, my little jokes on Thee,
And I'll forgive Thy great big one on me.
Robert Frost

PETS

SIT, KEWPIE! SIT, BLAST IT!
SIT!

© 1987 by NEA, Inc.

GLADYS!

The greatest pleasure of a dog is that you may make a fool of yourself with him and not only will he not scold you, but he will make a fool of himself too.

Samuel Butler

YOO-HOO, GLADYS, HAVE I GOT A SURPRISE FOR YOU!

YOU'LL NEVER GUESS WHAT THIS SUCKER DOWNTOWN SOLD ME FOR FIVE BUCKS...

?

...A HOMING PIGE—

!

MOST DOGS HAVE FLEAS... KEWPIE HAS MOTHS.

POLLY WANTS A CRACKER!
POLLY WANTS A CRACKER!
SO FEED TH' KID, ALREADY! WHAT D'YA EXPECT ME TO DO?
9-2

AH, KEWPIE, MY LOVE! AND WHAT KIND OF DAY DID YOU HAVE?
K
LOTS OF PEOPLE TALK TO ANIMALS, BUT **HE** WAITS FOR AN **ANSWER**.
1-17

If dogs could talk, perhaps we would find it as hard to get along with them as we do people.

Karel Capek

HIYA, WARREN!
HIDYDO, WILBERFORCE.
HEEL, BOY!
SANSOM

I DON'T GET IT?
THAT'S WARREN KARP AND HIS BROTHER...
© 1984 by NEA, Inc

THEY CAN'T AFFORD A PET.
11-21

WHAT'S WRONG WITH YOUR CANARY?
NOTHING...
...HE THINKS HE'S A BAT.
© 1983 by NEA, Inc. TM Reg U S Pat & TM Off
SANSOM
1-24

SKAT!
© 1988 by NEA, Inc

IF HE DIDN'T WANT A WATCHDOG, WHY DID HE BUY ONE?
KEWPIE

HAHA
CUTE PUPPY! HE JUMPED RIGHT ONTO MY LAP!

WHAT'S HIS NAME?
"NIAGARA"...

...Y'WANTA KNOW WHY?

A dog is the only thing on earth that loves you more than he loves himself.

Josh Billings

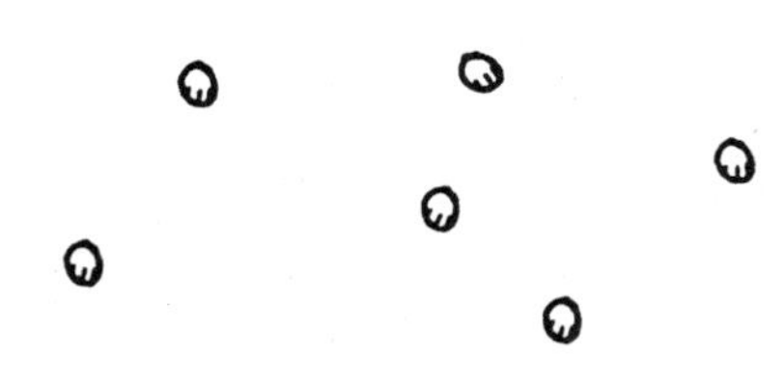

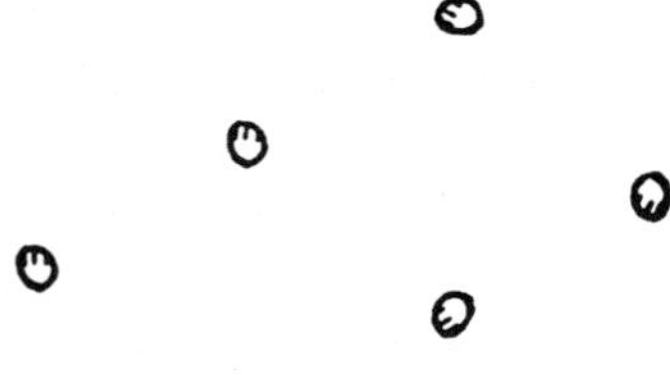

CAN YOU DIRECT ME TO THE LABRADORS?
END O' TH' CORRIDOR TO TH' RIGHT.
TERRIERS

DOG SHOW

DOG SHOW

LABRADOR RETRIEVERS!
TERRIERS
© 1983 by NEA, Inc. TM Reg U.S. Pat & TM Off
11-21

WHIMPER
WHINE
WOOF!

Z
10-8
© 1986 by NEA, Inc.

The dog who meets with a good master is the happier of the two.

Maurice Maeterlinck

I CAN'T BELIEVE IT....A GENUINE TALKING PARROT FOR ONLY $5!

SAY SOMETHING, BOY!

GRUM SCHMITKO GEVAULT DE DOODLEDINGDING SHMATSKE PALATZKO DOOB MULGOODNIK!
© 1980 by NEA, Inc. TM Reg U.S. Pat Off

HEEL, GIRL!

GOOD GIRL!

DON'T TELL ME OBEDIENCE SCHOOL DOESN'T PAY OFF!

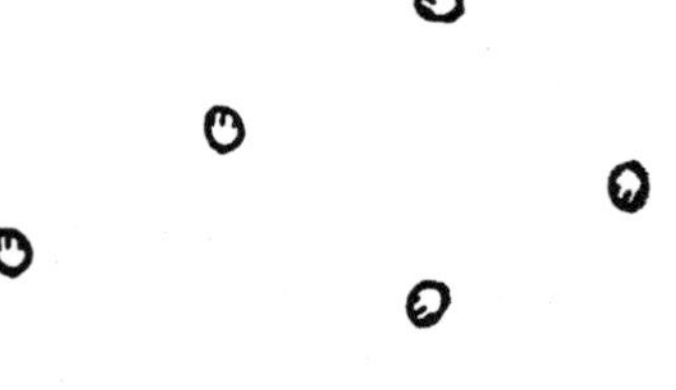

DINING OUT

MIGHT I SUGGEST CÔTE DE VEAU AU CURRY, DELICATELY SERVED WITH A RIZ CREOLE.
FINE, I'LL TAKE IT...
AND YOU MIGHT BRING A BOTTLE OF KETCHUP, TOO!
5-28

If you can't pronounce it, you can't afford it.
Dublin opinion,
quoted in Earl Wilson's column

GOOD EVENING, I'LL BE YOUR SERVER TONIGHT! MY NAME IS RAYMOND...
WELL, HOWDY, RAYMOND...MY NAME IS BRUTUS AND THIS IS MY WIFE, GLADYS, AND MY SON, WILBERFORCE.
SHEEEEEEEE!
© 1985 by NEA, Inc

© 1989 by NEA, Inc

PERHAPS IF YOU REMOVED THE CAP...

WINE, M'SIEUR?
UH, YEAH... ER, WHAT DO YOU SUGGEST?
CHATEAU CHEVROLET, '57!
FINE.
GLASS, OR BOTTLE?
BRING HIM A GLASS! DON'T YOU DARE DRINK OUT OF THE BOTTLE!
© 1986 by NEA, Inc
8-19
I'LL HAVE THE CHEF'S SALAD.
YOU SURE?
YES
HEY, LENNY, YOU EAT YOUR SALAD YET?
© 1986 by NEA, Inc.
4-11

No elegant restaurant can be better than the sense of excitement it conveys to women. Many women come to a fashionable place and act as if they were on stage.

Charles Ritz

...AND I CAN SAY WITHOUT FEAR OF CONTRADICTION...

WHAT CAN I GET YOU?

DO YOU HAVE A FRENCH DIP?

AS A MATTER OF FACT, WE DO.

OH, PIERRE!

Look here, steward, if this is coffee, I want tea;
but if this is tea, then I want coffee.

Punch

WHAT IS MONKFISH?
POOR MAN'S LOBSTER.
YOU GOT ANY POOR MAN'S MONKFISH?
© 1989 by NEA, Inc

WHAT'S THIS?
YOUR SALAD, SIR.
BUT I THOUGHT....?
HE ATE THE CENTERPIECE!
© 1985 by NEA, Inc

Tell me what you eat and I will tell you what you are!

Brillat-Savarin

HOW ABOUT LUNCH?
"ITALIAN" OKAY WITH YOU?
FINE!

SOUNDS GOOD TO ME!
WE'LL GO "DUTCH", OF COURSE.
© 1984 by NEA, Inc

I THOUGHT YOU SAID "ITALIAN"...
ART SANSOM 11-16

COCKTAILS?
BRING ME A DRY MARTINI WITH A TWIST.

I'LL HAVE THE SAME... AND MAKE CERTAIN THE GLASS IS CLEAN!
© 1983 by NEA, Inc. TM Reg U.S. Pat & TM Off

HERE Y'GO...UH... WHICH ONE OF YOU REQUESTED THE CLEAN GLASS?
ART SANSOM 12-21

I am not hungry; but, thank goodness, I am greedy!

Punch

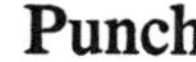

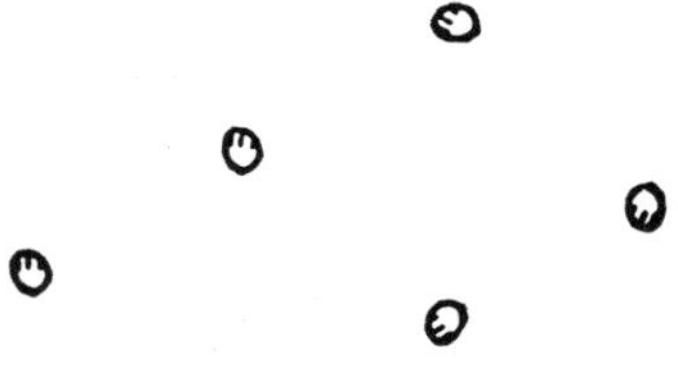

WE'LL EACH HAVE A PLUM DAIQUIRI!
DO YOU LADIES HAVE I.D.'S?
TEE-HEE... HERE YOU ARE!

SIGH... THE KNAVERY TO WHICH I MUST RESORT FOR MY 15%!
© 1986 by NEA, Inc.

THIS IS A VERY GOOD YEAR FOR THIS WINE!

WHAT YEAR IS IT?

LIKE I SAID... THIS YEAR!
© 1978 by NEA, Inc. T.M. Reg. U.S. Pat. Off.
8-21

THE FOOD HERE IS ONLY SO-SO, BUT THE SERVICE IS GREAT!

...AND WE'LL HAVE A BOTTLE OF YOUR BEST WINE.

HEY, SAL, ONE VINO... THE SEEDLESS KIND!

BURP
I'M BUYING YOU LUNCH, WASTREL... DON'T EMBARRASS ME!
© 1988 by NEA, Inc

HOW WOULD YOU LIKE YOUR STEAKS?
MEDIUM
ART/CHIP SANSOM 9-22

LARGE!

POP!

WOULD M'SIEUR CARE TO EXAMINE THE BOUQUET?
© 1987 by NEA, Inc
ART/CHIP SANSOM 7-21

Grub first, then ethics.
Bertold Brecht

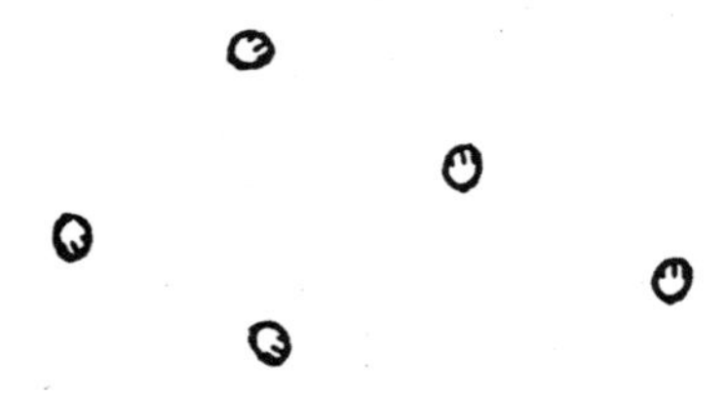

ZAP

ZAP
ZAP

ZAP
ZAP
ZAP

KETCHUP?
8-19 (c) 1985 by NEA Inc

SORRY, SIR, THERE'S A 40-MINUTE WAIT FOR A TABLE.
HMM... I DO BELIEVE YOU DROPPED THIS PORTRAIT OF ALEXANDER HAMILTON...
6-5
© 1985 by NEA Inc
?

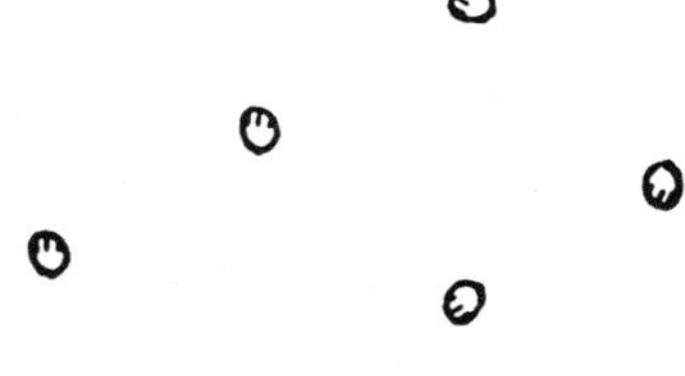

WHO DID YOU SAY RECOMMENDED THIS PLACE?

AW, FOR... LOOK, IF YOU WANT MY CHOCOLATE MOUSSE, ASK FOR IT!

GIVE ME YOUR CHOCOLATE MOUSSE.

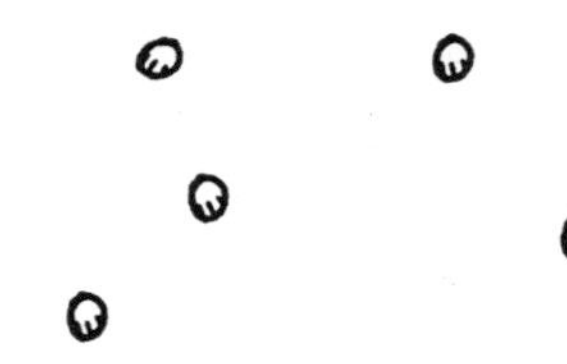

HEALTH

COMPREHEND, DIVIDE, CONQUER!
INTEGRITY, TRADITION...
PRIDE OF CRAFTSMANSHIP!
ASSIMILATE, EVALUATE, GROW!
HEADACHE, ACID INDIGESTION, HEARTBURN, COMMON SYMPTOMS OF NEURALGIA...
BUS
© 1986 by NEA, Inc.

Some people think that doctors and nurses can put scrambled eggs back in the shell.
Dorothy Canfield

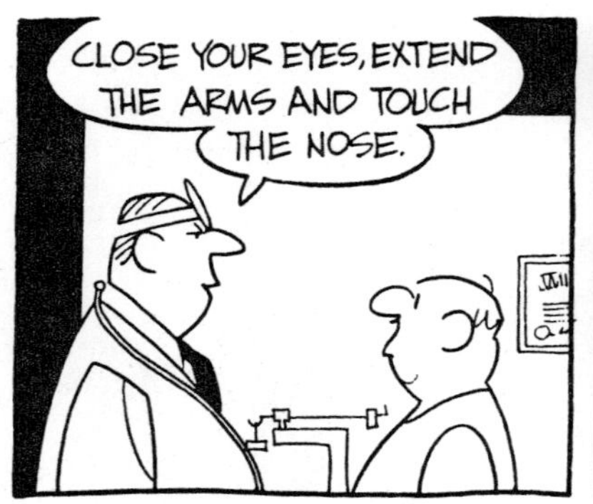
CLOSE YOUR EYES, EXTEND THE ARMS AND TOUCH THE NOSE.

© 1986 by NEA, Inc.
Chip Sansom 12-29

TIME FOR OUR ANNUAL BOOSTER SHOT, EH? WELL, DON'T FRET, LITTLE LADY...

I PROMISE THIS WILL HURT ME AS MUCH AS YOU...

© 1983 by NEA, Inc. TM Reg U.S. Pat & TM Off
AND YOU CAN HOLD ME TO THAT!
Sansom 4-22

Joy, temperance, and repose
Slam the door on the doctor's nose.
Longfellow

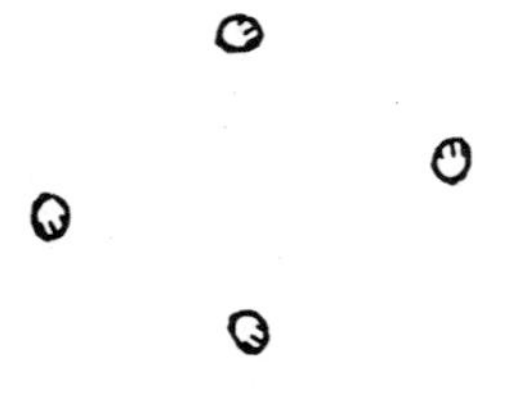

INEZ HAS BAD NEWS ABOUT COUSIN NORBITT!
THAT HYPOCHONDRIAC THINKS HE'S GOT SOME TERRIBLE NEW AILMENT EVERY MONTH!
IT'S WORSE THIS TIME... NOW HE THINKS HE'S DEAD.

I WANT A BOTTLE OF PYRIDOXINEHYDROCHLORIDE.
?
OH... YOU WANT VITAMIN B6!
YEAH, THAT'S IT! I NEVER CAN REMEMBER THAT NAME.

The report of my death was an exaggeration.
Mark Twain

I'VE GOT GOOD NEWS AND BAD NEWS... FIRST THE BAD NEWS...

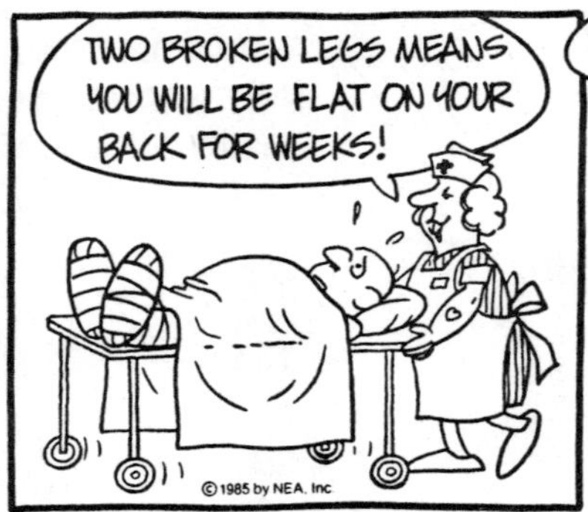
TWO BROKEN LEGS MEANS YOU WILL BE FLAT ON YOUR BACK FOR WEEKS!
©1985 by NEA, Inc

THE GOOD NEWS IS MR. ECCLESTONE HERE WANTS TO BUY YOUR SLIPPERS!

YOU ARE NOW IN A DEEP SLEEP...
© 1983 by NEA, Inc. TM Reg U S Pat & TM Off

WHEN YOU AWAKEN, YOU WILL NEVER AGAIN DESIRE A CIGARETTE...

AND YOU WILL MAKE ME A GIFT OF YOUR GOLD LIGHTER.

HMM... IT'S NOT A MOLE...

IT LOOKS LIKE... YES...

...YOU HAVE THE MEASLE!

MY GREAT-GRANDFATHER RODE A HORSE, BUT WOULDN'T GO NEAR A TRAIN...

GRANDPA RODE IN TRAINS, BUT WAS AFRAID OF AUTOMOBILES...

POP DROVE A CAR ALL HIS LIFE, BUT WAS AFRAID TO FLY...

I LOVE TO FLY, BUT I'M AFRAID TO RIDE A HORSE...
MAIL

At fifty, everyone has the face he deserves.
George Orwell

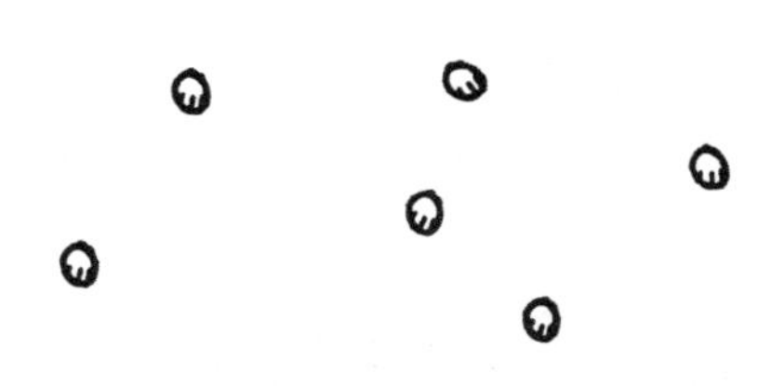

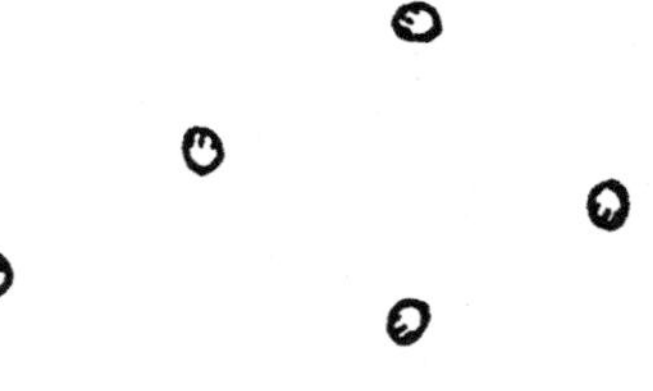

OH, YES, MY BABY IS IN HIS THIRD YEAR OF MEDICAL SCHOOL!

HE'S MAJORING IN GERIATRICS, YOU KNOW!

WELL, HERE'S HOPING HE'LL BE THE ONE TO FIND A CURE FOR IT SOMEDAY.
5-29

NOW, LITTLE LADY, SAY "AH!"
NO.
PRETTY PLEASE?
NO!

AH!
© 1986 by NEA, Inc.

The best way to get the better of temptation is just to yield to it.

Clementina Stirling Graham

I NEVER SMOKED, BOOZED OR CHASED WIMMIN!
© 1984 by NEA, Inc.

HAVEN'T ET RED MEAT IN 39 YEAR, AM ASLEEP BY NINE EVER NIGHT AND JUST CELEBRATED M'NINETIETH BIRTHDAY!

HOW?
8-28
ART SANSOM

THEY SAID IT COULDN'T BE DONE, BUT WITHIN ME I KNEW I MIGHT...

SO I TRIED AND TRIED AND TRIED AND TRIED...
© 1985 by NEA, Inc

AND YOU KNOW WHAT? THEY WERE RIGHT!
ART SANSOM 9-17

Abstainer—A weak person who yields to the temptation of denying himself a pleasure.
Ambrose Bierce

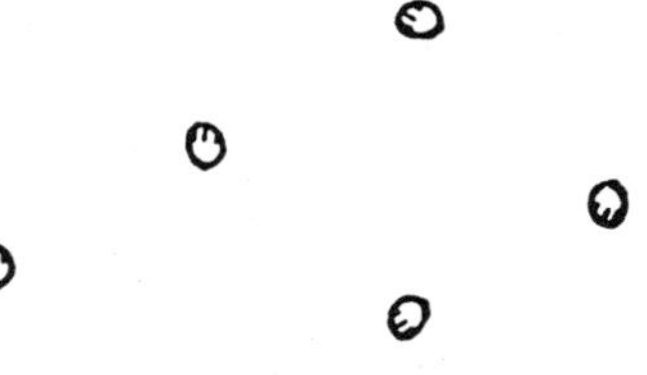

MARRIAGE

SIGH...WHEN WE WERE YOUNG, A DATE WITH BRUTUS MEANT FAST CARS AND ORIENTAL FOOD...

5-16

NOW IT'S ORIENTAL CARS AND FAST FOOD!
DRIVE-IN WINDOW
©1986 by NEA, Inc.

The most dangerous food is a wedding cake.
American proverb

GET OUT YOUR FRILLIEST FROCK, LOVER, WE'RE GOING OUT FOR OUR ANNIVERSARY DINNER!

ACTUALLY, I'D SORT OF PLANNED ON A NICE, ROMANTIC EVENING AT HOME, ALONE.

NONSENSE! I'M NOT GOING OUT TO DINNER BY MYSELF!
©1986 by NEA, Inc
10-10

©1982 by NEA, Inc. TM Reg U S Pat & TM Off

HOW MANY TIMES HAVE I TOLD YOU, THAT'S NOT FUNNY!?
10-13

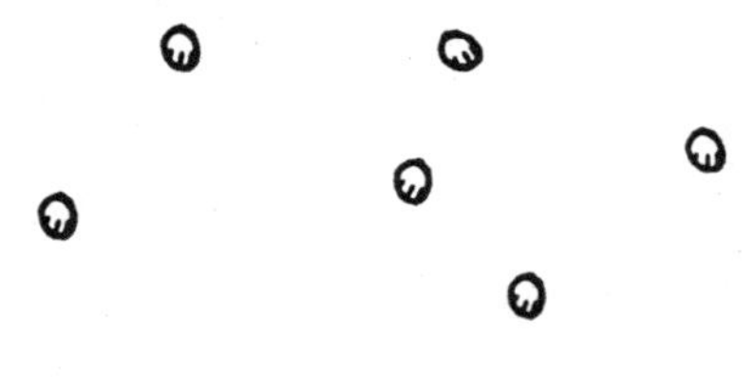

TELL ME I'M NOT GETTING OLD AND DOWDY!

OKAY, YOU'RE NOT GETTING OLD AND DOWDY.
© 1980 by NEA, Inc. T M Reg U S Pat Off

YOU'RE JUST SAYING THAT.
4-25

MM...ROMANTIC, ISN'T IT!
YAWN
© 1989 by NEA, Inc

Z Z Z
!

HE STILL LIKES TO PARK, BUT HE'S FORGOTTEN WHY!
4-6

The woman cries before the wedding; the man after.

Polish proverb

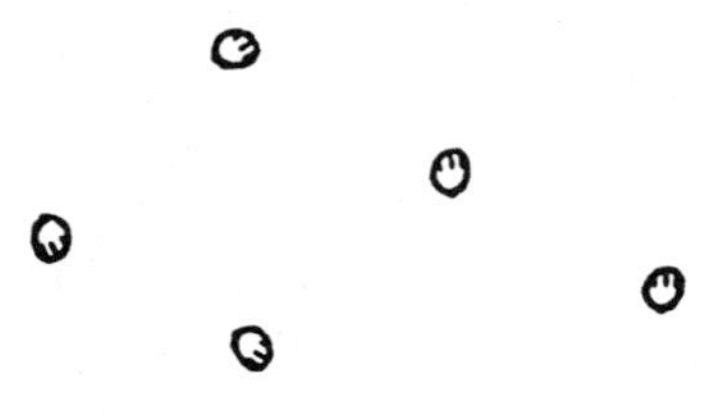

OH, I DON'T KNOW, GLADYS...

...TAKE AWAY HIS PROFILE, HIS RICH, BARITONE VOICE AND HIS IMPOSING 6'-4" HEIGHT AND WHAT'VE YOU GOT?
© 1988 by NEA, Inc.

YOU.

© 1983 by NEA, Inc., TM Reg. U.S. Pat & TM Off.
OUCH!
HOLD IT, GLADYS!
WHAT'VE YOU GOT AGAINST GOING TO A MARRIAGE COUNSELOR?

Love lessens a woman's delicacy and increases a man's.

La Bruyere

YES, I FOUND A WALLET THAT MAY BE YOURS... CAN YOU IDENTIFY ITS CONTENTS?
IT CONTAINED $37 AND A PICTURE OF MY WIFE.
HMM... THAT'S RIGHT. ARE YOU OFFERING A REWARD?
YOU MAY KEEP THE PICTURE OF MY WIFE.

WITH ALL HIS SHORTCOMINGS, BRUTUS HAS BEEN A LOYAL AND FAITHFUL HUSBAND.
I THINK...
AND IF HE HASN'T, WHO CARES, RIGHT?

Men should keep their eyes wide open before marriage, and half shut afterward.
Madame Scuderi

WHAT DOES THAT BIG CLOUD REMIND YOU OF?
JUST A CLOUD.

COME ON, DON'T YOU HAVE ANY IMAGINATION?
I GUESS IT KINDA LOOKS LIKE A TURTLE WITH A TELEPHONE ON ITS BACK.

THAT'S THE DUMBEST THING I EVER HEARD!
© 1985 by NEA, Inc.
4-5

GLADYS, AM I... ERUDITE?
SURE.
WHY?

BECAUSE.
BUT WHY BECAUSE?
LOOK, I'M NOT SURE I KNOW WHAT ERUDITE MEANS.
IT MEANS SCHOLARLY.
4-26

NO.

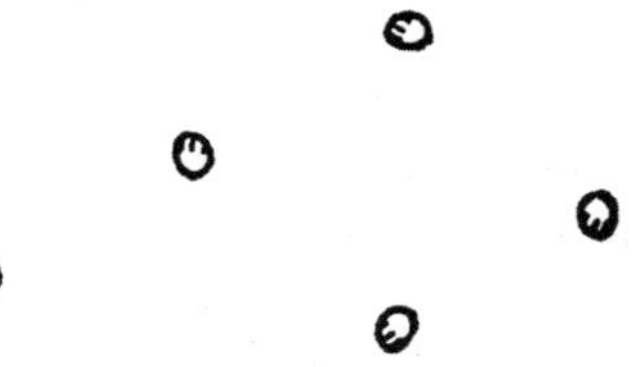

GEE, I'M GOING TO MISS MAMA WHEN SHE'S AWAY VISITING AUNT FRANCES...

I ALWAYS LOOK FORWARD TO OUR "TALKIE TIMES".
CAN'T YOU TALK TO ME?

NO
WHY NOT?

YOU'RE WHAT WE TALK ABOUT.
© 1987 by NEA, Inc.

KISS

BLOW

STILL MAD AT ME, AREN'T YOU?
© 1983 by NEA, Inc. TM Reg U S Pat & TM Off

Marriage! Nothing else demands so much of a man!

Ibsen

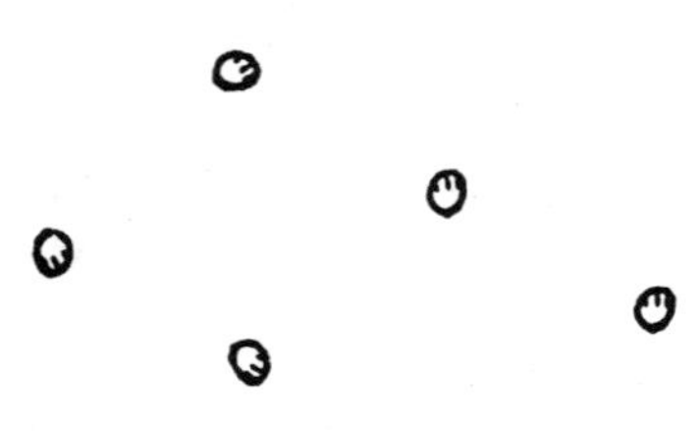

SOB ...I WANT TO REPORT A MISSING HUSBAND...HIS NAME IS BRUTUS ...HE'S FIVE-FEET-FOUR...
12
...HE'S BALD, BOWLEGGED, PAUNCHY, HAS FLAT FEET, POOR TABLE MANNERS...
12
...A NEGATIVE PERSONALITY, WOBBLY DENTURES..........
ON SECOND THOUGHT, FORGET IT!
7-21 © 1984 by NEA Inc

I DON'T CARE TO DISCUSS THE SUBJECT!

© 1983 by NEA, Inc. TM Reg U.S. Pat & TM Off

DID YOU HEAR ME?

The best for a man and the best for a woman is not the same.

Ortega y Gasset

HOLD ON, NOW, HERE'S ANOTHER ONE...STOP ME IF YOU'VE HEARD IT!
© 1978 by NEA, Inc., T.M. Reg. U.S. Pat. Off.

OH, GLORY, HAVE YOU EVER SEEN A MORE ROMANTIC MOON?
© 1988 by NEA, Inc.

WHAT A PERFECT MOMENT FOR A POEM... DO YOU KNOW ONE?

THERE WAS AN OLD MAN FROM DUBUQUE...

Woman inspires us to great things, and prevents us from achieving them.

Alexander Dumas

EDUCATION

DO YOU HAVE ANY CHILDREN WHO ARE BEING "BUSED"?
ONE CHILD.
DO YOU FEEL THAT BUSING IS ACHIEVING ITS PURPOSE?
NO...
...THEY KEEP BRINGING HIM BACK.
ART SANSOM 10-1
© 1984 by NEA, Inc.

It takes lots of things to prove you are smart, but only one thing to prove you are ignorant.

Don Herold

THERE SHE GOES, THE MOST UNDISCI-PLINED WILDCAT WE'VE EVER HAD.
24 25 26 27 28 29 30

SHE DISRUPTS CLASSES AND JUST WREAKS HAVOC IN GENERAL! BUT TO COMPOUND MATTERS...
© 1984 by NEA Inc

...SHE HAS A PERFECT ATTENDANCE RECORD.

TODAY THINGS ARE GONNA BE DIFFERENT, BOY! TODAY I'M NOT GETTIN' INTO ANY TROUBLE!

RISE AND SHINE, WILBERFORCE, YOU'LL BE LATE FOR SCHOOL!
© 1985 by NEA, Inc

WHO'S GOIN'!?

You know . . . everybody is ignorant, only on different subjects.

Will Rogers

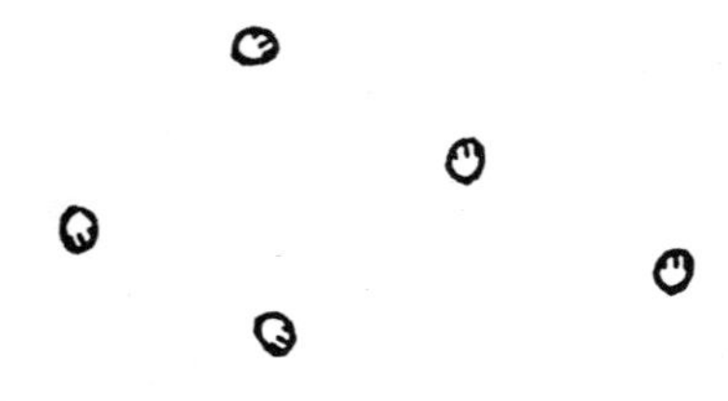

HURRICANE, SPELL "TURKEY"!
©1982 by NEA, Inc., TM Reg. U.S. Pat. & TM Off
TURKEY LIKE IN THANKSGIVING OR LIKE IN WILMA SCHLOCK'S BROTHER?
11-13

SO YOU FIGURE YOU'VE HAD ENOUGH EDUCATION! WELL, LET'S JUST SEE HOW SMART YOU ARE!

WHO WAS OUR FIRST PRESIDENT?
GEORGE WASHINGTON.

AND THE SECOND?
JOHN ADAMS.
AND....JUST A MINUTE...

WHO WAS THIRD?
©1985 by NEA, Inc.
7-30

Strange how much you've got to know before you know how little you know.

Anonymous

THERE WERE TWO
APPLES ON MY
DESK, CLASS, AND
ONE OF THEM
IS MISSING...

NOW I AM TURNING
MY BACK AND I
EXPECT WHOEVER
TOOK THE APPLE
TO RETURN IT.
© 1978 by NEA, Inc., T.M. Reg. U.S. Pat. Off.
SANSOM
10-2

I ASSURE YOU
NOTHING MORE
WILL BE SAID
ABOUT THE
MATTER.

OH, YEAH, WELL, I'VE GOT
NEWS FOR YOU...

A VERBAL AGREEMENT ISN'T
WORTH THE PAPER IT'S WRITTEN
ON!

...........WATCHING "DING-DONG
SCHOOL" SEEMS TO BE PAYING
OFF FOR HIM.
SANSOM
12-9
© 1985 by NEA, Inc

Ignorance is preferable to error.
Thomas Jefferson

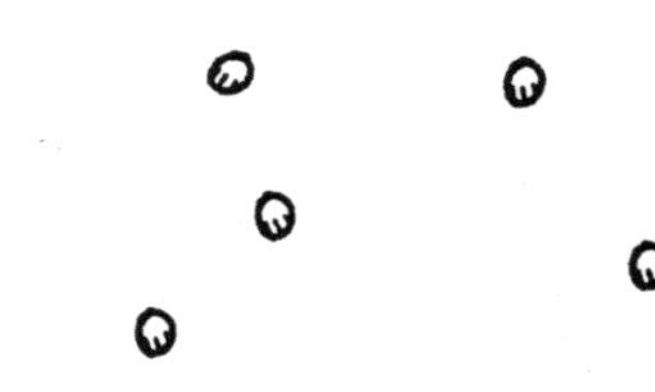

HURRICANE, WHAT DOES 3+4 EQUAL?
3+4=3+4

CLASS, YOU MAY BE EXCUSED FOR RECESS.
© 1979 by NEA, Inc. T.M. Reg. U.S. Pat. Off.

THE WEIRD PART IS THAT ALL HER ANSWERS MAKE SENSE...

NOW THEN, WHO CAN DEFINE "LIGHT YEAR"... YES, HURRICANE?
SAME AS A REGULAR, BUT LESS CALORIES?
© 1980 by NEA, Inc.

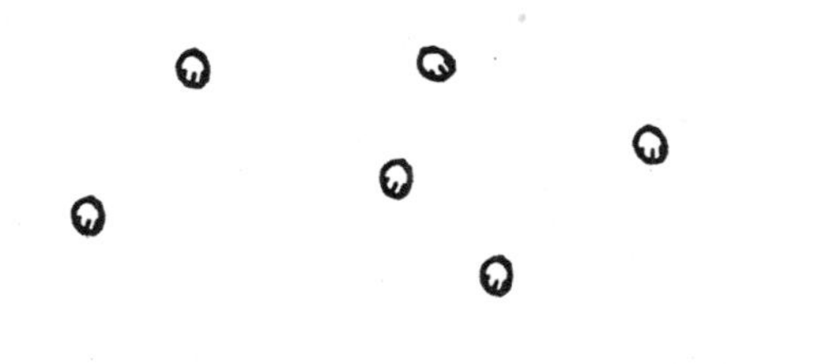

HE KEPT LEARNING MORE AND MORE...

...ABOUT LESS AND LESS...
© 1987 by NEA, Inc.

...TILL HE KNOWS EVERYTHING ABOUT NOTHING.

WHY ARE YOU SO UPSET WITH THE BOY?

THIS REPORT CARD IS A REAL IMPROVEMENT!
© 1990 by NEA, Inc. T.M. Reg U.S. Pat Off

IT SHOULD BE...THEY MADE HIM TAKE THE SAME SUBJECTS OVER.

A good education is the next best thing to a pushy mother.

Charles Schulz

MONEY

THIS IS A GREAT OPPORTUNITY FOR YOU, MY BOY, WITH TRAVEL AND PRESTIGE, NOT TO MENTION MORE MONEY!
© 1984 by NEA Inc. TM Reg U S Pat & TM Off
UH, HOW MUCH MORE MONEY?

I SAID NOT TO MENTION MORE MONEY!
3-14

Money is always there, but the pockets change.
Gertrude Stein

IT'S A TIGHT ECONOMY, GLADYS, AND WE'RE GOING TO CUT A LOT OF CORNERS! FOR STARTERS, WE'LL USE THE TV FOR ONLY THREE HOURS EACH DAY...
THE OLD CAR WILL HAVE TO LAST ANOTHER FIVE YEARS, YOUR HOUSKEEPING ALLOWANCE WILL BE CUT 25%, INSTEAD OF FLORIDA THIS WINTER...
...I'LL BUY A SUN LAMP, AND WILBERFORCE'S TEETH WILL HAVE TO WAIT TO BE STRAIGHTENED! NOW WHAT ARE YOU WILLING TO GIVE UP?
YOU.
ART/CHIP SANSOM 9-29

MR. O'HARA DOESN'T MAKE HURRICANE SHOVEL THE SNOW!
MR. O'HARA DOESN'T PAY YOUR ALLOWANCE EVERY WEEK!
NEITHER DO YOU.

Two can live as cheap as one, but it costs twice as much.

Anonymous

BOY, ANOTHER LOTTERY WINNER... THIS GUY GETS $26,000,000! WHY CAN'T I HAVE THAT KIND OF LUCK?!
TRY CHANGING YOUR LUCK BY BUYING YOUR TICKET SOMEWHERE ELSE.
TICKET?
© 1987 by NEA, Inc
5-25

The LITTLE LOAN CO.
"DEALING ON A PERSONAL LEVEL"

WELL, MR. THORNAPPLE, YOUR REFERENCES ARE EXCELLENT AND YOUR RECORDS SEEM TO BE IN ORDER...
© 1982 by NEA, Inc. TM Reg U.S. Pat & TM Off

...BUT, QUITE FRANKLY, I DON'T LIKE YOUR LOOKS.
10-22

A rich man is nothing but a poor man with money.

W.C. Fields

AND WHAT DO WE WANT FOR OUR BIRTHDAY? A BABY DOLL? SKATES? A PUPPY DOG?

A CREDIT CARD.
ART SANSOM 9-23

YOU CAN BUY A SET OF FIVE OF THESE PUNCTURE-PROOF TIRES FOR A LOW-LOW $300!
WHY FIVE TIRES?
FOR A SPARE!
IF THEY'RE PUNCTURE-PROOF, WHY DO WE NEED A SPARE?
Bill
Bill
ART/CHIP SANSOM © 1989 by NEA Inc
3-13

I hate money, but it soothes my nerves.
Joe Louis

MY NEW ROLLS IS MAGNIFICENT, BUT I DON'T LIKE TO APPEAR OSTENTATIOUS...

I MISS THE SIMPLE, MUNDANE STATEMENT MY OLD CAR MADE.
© 1988 by NEA, Inc.

THE MERCEDES?
CHECK
1-22

$50 AN **OUNCE**? THAT'S **RIDICULOUS**!

LET'S SEE... HMM... OKAY, I'LL TAKE $2 WORTH.
YOU JUST DID.
© 1983 by NEA, Inc. TM Reg U S Pat & TM Off
4/25

If you want to know what a man is really like, make notice how he acts when he loses money.

New England proverb

LOSE SOMETHING?
MY LUCKY SILVER DOLLAR...

FIND IT AND I'LL GIVE YOU A NICKEL.
OH, WOW!
PSST! HEY, KID...

HUH?
I'LL GIVE YOU A DIME FOR IT.
© 1979 by NEA, Inc. T.M. Reg. U.S. Pat. Off.
8-21

AS A VALUED CUSTOMER, I AM CALLING YOU PERSONALLY TO SAY YOUR ACCOUNT IS OVERDRAWN IN THE AMOUNT OF $78.

OH, DEARIE ME, I'LL PUT A CHECK IN THE MAIL TODAY!

BUT, MRS. THORNAPPLE !
MRS. THORNAPPLE?
HELLO?
© 1984 by NEA, Inc
1-3-85

If you want to make money, go where the money is.

Joseph P. Kennedy

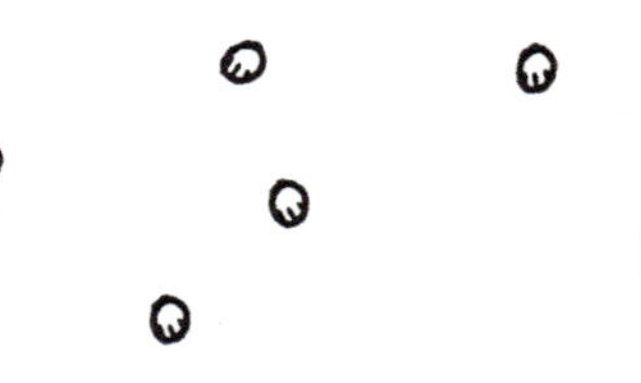

SOCIAL MATTERS

AND NOW, A MAN WHO NEEDS NO INTRODUCTION...
LET'S HAVE A WARM WELCOME FOR---
BRUTUS THORNAPPLE!
© 1984 by NEA, Inc.

The world is a stage, but the play is badly cast.
Shakespeare

A MR. THORNAPPLE TO SEE YOU...
LET HIM WAIT!

I CANNOT ABIDE PEOPLE WHO COME CALLING DURING THE DINNER HOUR!

YES, THORNAPPLE, WHAT IN TARNATION IS IT?!
YOU INVITED ME TO DINNER.
© 1982 by NEA, Inc. TM Reg U.S. Pat. & TM Off

HEY, GOOD-LOOKIN', HOWZABOUT A LITTLE KISS!

I DARE YOU TO STEP OUTSIDE AND SAY THAT!
© 1984 by NEA Inc

I MEANT **HER**, NOT YOU, WEIRDO!

We're all in this alone.

Lily Tomlin

OH, YEAH?
YEAH!
YEAH?
YEAH?
YEAH!
YEAH!
7-3
SHOULDN'T WE STOP THEM?
OH, LET 'EM FIGHT...
THEY CAN'T HURT EACH OTHER.
© 1985 by NEA inc

EVER HAD SUSHI BEFORE?
NO, IT LOOKS A LITTLE YUCKY...

BUT IT TASTES KINDA LIKE FISH.
8-9
© 1985 by NEA inc

HA-HA, BRUTUS, YOU CRACK ME UP!

AND YOU SAID I WASN'T FUNNY.
© 1980 by NEA, Inc. TM Reg U S Pat Off

ON THE CONTRARY... I SAID, YOU DON'T HAVE A SENSE OF HUMOR.

MR. VEEBLEFESTER AND I HAVE BEEN DISCUSSING THE IMPRESSIONISTS.
© 1988 by NEA Inc.

ARE YOU PARTIAL TO MONET OR RENOIR?

ACTUALLY I LIKE RICH LITTLE MYSELF.

Life is far too serious a thing to ever talk seriously about.

Oscar Wilde

©1983 by NEA. Inc . TM Reg U S Pat & TM Off
10-24

HA-HA, IT SEEMS SIX MORONS WERE SITTING AROUND TALKING...

THERE WAS DO, RE, FA, SOL, LA AND TI...
AREN'T YOU FORGETTING "MI"?
©1985 by NEA Inc

OH, DID I OVERLOOK YOU?
8-29

Nobody can ever make you feel inferior without your consent.

Eleanor Roosevelt

SHALL WE RETIRE TO THE LIBRARY FOR BRANDY AND CIGARS?
© 1983 by NEA, Inc. TM Reg U S Pat & TM Off

OH, GOLLY, I THINK IT CLOSES AT SEVEN...
2-11

I DON'T GET IT...
© 1982 by NEA, Inc., TM Reg. U.S. Pat. & TM Off
8/21

Always leave them laughing when you say goodbye.

George M. Cohan

The End?